National Transportation Safety Board
Fiscal Year 2014 and 2013
Performance and Accountability Report

**National
Transportation
Safety Board**

THE NATIONAL TRANSPORTATION SAFETY BOARD AT A GLANCE

Established, April 1, 1967

Headquarters

490 L'Enfant Plaza, SW
Washington, DC 20594
www.ntsb.gov

FY 2014 Budget: $103.0 million

Full Time Equivalent Employees: 402

How to use this Report

This Performance and Accountability Report (PAR) for fiscal year (FY) 2014 and 2013 provides financial and performance information for the National Transportation Safety Board (NTSB) that enables the President, the Congress, and the American people to assess the agency's performance as required by the following legislation:

- Government Performance and Results Act Modernization Act (GPRAMA) of 2010
- Accountability of Tax Dollars Act of 2002
- Government Management Reform Act of 1994
- Government Performance and Results Act (GPRA) of 1993
- Chief Financial Officers Act of 1990
- Federal Manager's Financial Integrity Act (FMFIA) of 1982
- Office of Management and Budget (OMB) Circular A-11
- Office of Management and Budget (OMB) Circular A-136

This report compares performance results to the agency's strategic and performance goals. The NTSB's Strategic Plan and annual PARs are available on the NTSB's website at http://www.ntsb.gov/about/reports.html. The NTSB welcomes feedback on the form and content of this report.

This report is organized as follows:

Introduction
This section includes a message from the Acting Chairman attesting to the reliability and completeness of the financial and performance information presented in the report and includes a statement of assurance of the agency's management controls as required by the FMFIA. This section also discusses NTSB's role in transportation safety.

Management's Discussion and Analysis (MD&A)
This section provides an overview of the financial and performance information contained in the Performance and Financial sections and appendixes. The MD&A includes an overview of the NTSB organization, highlights of the agency's performance goals and results, the current status of systems and internal control weaknesses, and other pertinent information.

Performance Section
This section provides annual performance information as required by OMB Circular A-11, the GPRA, the GPRAMA, and includes a detailed discussion and analysis of the agency's performance in FY 2014. It also includes information about past results of key performance measures.

Financial Section
This section contains a message from the Chief Financial Officer, details of the NTSB's FY 2014 finances, and includes the Department of Transportation's Office of the Inspector General (DOT/OIG) Quality Control Report, the Independent Auditor's Report, the NTSB Chief Financial Officer's Response to the Auditor's Report, the agency's audited financial statements, and notes to the financial statements.

LEGISLATIVE MANDATE

Maintaining our congressionally mandated independence and objectivity;

Conducting objective, precise accident investigations and safety studies;

Performing fair and objective airman and mariner certification appeals;

Advocating and promoting safety recommendations; and,

Assisting victims of transportation accidents and their families.

MISSION/VISION

To be a Premier Organization Improving Transportation Safety

CORE VALUES

We are committed to the core values:

Safety,
Excellence,
Independence,
Integrity,
Diversity and Inclusion,
Transparency

STRATEGIC GOALS

Strategic Goal No. 1: *Conduct Effective Accident Investigations.*

Strategic Goal No. 2: *Recommend and Advocate Actions to Improve Global Transportation Safety.*

Strategic Goal No. 3: *Conduct Fair and Expeditious Adjudication of Airman and Mariner Appeals from the Federal Aviation Administration and the US Coast Guard Enforcement Actions and Certificate Denials.*

Strategic Goal No. 4: *Provide Outstanding Mission Support.*

Table of Contents

Introduction

A Message from the Acting Chairman

I am pleased to present the National Transportation Safety Board's (NTSB) FY 2014 Annual Performance and Accountability Report. This report highlights the agency's mission, reflects the expansion of our core values, and details our strategic goal priorities, accomplishments, and challenges in upholding our mission to promote transportation safety. It also provides an accounting to the American people on our stewardship of the funding we received from them for FY 2014 to ensure the fulfillment of our mission. This report contains the NTSB's financial statements, as required by OMB Circular A-136, a selection of annual performance information, and a report on the NTSB's internal controls, as required by the Federal Manager's Financial Integrity Act (FMFIA).

The NTSB is recognized internationally for its accident investigation experience, and also for issuing, advancing, and closing safety recommendations. For more than 40 years, the NTSB's dedicated staff have achieved excellence at the forefront of transportation safety issues. We aim to continually stimulate and promote beneficial change within the transportation community—change that helps to fulfill, and is consistent with, our mission and core values.

Leon Snead & Company, P.C., an independent public accounting firm engaged by the Department of Transportation's Office of Inspector General, audited the NTSB's FY 2014 consolidated financial statements included in this report and issued an unmodified (clean) opinion, indicating that our statements fairly present the financial position of the NTSB. This marks the NTSB's achievement of 12 consecutive unmodified opinions and is the best possible audit result, further affirming our commitment to financial reporting excellence.

I am also pleased to report on the NTSB's compliance with the FMFIA and the revised OMB Circular A-123 "Management's Responsibility for Internal Control" as of September 30, 2014. The FMFIA requires the NTSB to annually evaluate its management controls and identify any material weaknesses. This requirement covers all agency programs and administrative functions.

As we work to serve the American people, we must administer our programs as efficiently and economically as possible. To do this, we rely on our system of management controls to provide reasonable assurance that our financial activities comply with applicable laws, our items of value are safeguarded, and our operations are accounted for properly.

As of September 30, 2014, there are no new material weaknesses to report and the sole prior year weakness has been corrected. The corrected material weakness is NTSB's compliance with "Internal Controls over Financial Reporting."

Additionally, the NTSB has implemented leading management practices in all areas where the Government Accountability Office (GAO) made prior recommendations. These areas include (1) communication, strategic planning, information technology, knowledge management, organizational structure, human capital management, training, and financial management; (2) increasing the efficiency of activities related to investigating accidents, issuing recommendations, and conducting safety studies; and (3) increasing the use of our Training Center. We have also made substantial progress in developing an effective strategy for utilizing the data produced by our labor cost accounting system.

The performance goals and accomplishments in this report summarize our success in achieving the strategic goals we established for FY 2014. Over the past several fiscal years, our performance-based culture has been a focus of agency management and staff; it will continue to be enhanced in future years, as our measures and targets are revised, tracked, and evaluated.

We look forward to continuing to serve the Congress and the public as we reach our financial management and performance goals, while addressing current and future challenges in advancing transportation safety.

Sincerely,

/s/

Christopher A. Hart
Acting Chairman
November 1, 2014

The NTSB's Vital Role in Transportation Safety

The National Transportation Safety Board (NTSB) is an independent federal agency responsible for investigating and determining the probable cause of every civil aviation accident in the United States and significant accidents in other modes of transportation—railroad, highway, marine, and pipeline. With this vested responsibility, the NTSB develops recommendations that will prevent future accidents or reduce their effects in terms of injury, loss of life, or damage to property.

The NTSB promotes transportation safety, assists victims of transportation accidents and their families, conducts safety studies, and prepares accident reports based on investigation and analyses of transportation accident and incident data. NTSB investigations are used to determine factors common to a series of events and to identify safety improvements or evaluate the worth of transportation related devices or policies. Safety studies enhance the NTSB's corporate knowledge, enabling it to better perform its transportation safety mission.

Since its inception in 1967, the NTSB has investigated more than 140,500 aviation accidents and thousands of surface transportation accidents. On call 24 hours a day, 365 days a year, NTSB investigators have traveled throughout the country and to every corner of the world. Thanks to this dedication, the NTSB is recognized as the world's leading accident investigation agency.

The NTSB has issued more than 14,000 safety recommendations to more than 2,300 recipients in all transportation modes as a result of its investigations. Since 1990, the NTSB has published a Most Wanted List of transportation safety improvements, highlighting safety-critical actions that the US Department of Transportation (DOT) modal administrations, the US Coast Guard (USCG), and others should take to help prevent accidents and save lives. The NTSB does not have authority to regulate transportation equipment, personnel, or operations, or to initiate enforcement action. However, based on its reputation for objectivity and thoroughness, the NTSB has achieved such success in shaping transportation safety judgments that those who are in a position to affect transportation safety changes have accepted more than 74 percent of the agency's recommendations. Many safety features currently in airplanes, helicopters, automobiles, commercial motor vehicles, trains, pipelines, and marine vessels had their genesis in NTSB recommendations.

The NTSB meets its important safety mission through several lines of business that work together to prevent future accidents. These lines of business are:

Office of Aviation Safety (AS): The mission of AS is to accomplish the following: (1) Investigate all air carrier, commuter, and air taxi accidents; in-flight collisions; fatal and nonfatal general aviation accidents; and certain public aircraft accidents; (2) Participate in the investigation of major airline crashes in foreign countries that involve US carriers, US-manufactured or -designed equipment, or US-registered aircraft to fulfill US obligations under International Civil Aviation Organization agreements; and (3) Conduct investigations concerning safety issues that extend beyond a single accident to examine specific aviation safety problems from a broader perspective.

AS is responsible for investigating domestic aviation accidents and incidents (about 1,750 annually) and for proposing probable causes for the Board's approval. Working with other offices within the NTSB, AS develops recommendations to prevent the recurrence of similar accidents and incidents, and to otherwise improve aviation safety.

AS conducts investigative activities through five specialty divisions based in Washington, DC, and a regional investigation management structure consisting of four regional office sites. Investigators are located throughout the country, including Hawaii. International aviation activities are coordinated from the Washington, DC office.

Office of Highway Safety (HS): The Office of Highway Safety (HS) investigates accidents that have a significant impact on public confidence in highway transportation safety, highlight national safety issues, or generate high public interest and media attention. Such accidents may include collapses of highway bridge or tunnel structures, mass casualties and injuries on public transportation vehicles (such as motorcoaches and school buses), collisions at highway–rail grade crossings, and accidents that involve new safety issues or technologies. In addition, HS conducts studies based on trends emerging from NTSB accident investigations and from other research and accident data to identify common risks or underlying causes of accidents. To accomplish these tasks, HS is organized into two primary units: the Investigations Division and the Report Development Division.

Office of Marine Safety (MS): The Office of Marine Safety (MS) investigates major marine accidents on or under the territorial waters of the United States, including accidents involving US merchant vessels and those involving both US public and nonpublic vessels in the same casualty. In addition, the office investigates selected catastrophic marine accidents or those of a recurring nature.

The USCG conducts preliminary investigations of all marine accidents and notifies the NTSB if an accident qualifies as a major marine casualty, which is defined as resulting in at least one of the following:

- Six or more fatalities.
- Loss of a self-propelled vessel of 100 or more gross tons.
- Property damage of more than $500,000.
- Serious threat to life, property, or the environment as a result of hazardous materials.

MS investigates and determines the probable cause of all major marine casualties. For select major marine casualties, the office launches a full investigative team and presents the investigative product to the Board. All other major marine casualties are investigated by the USCG on behalf of the NTSB, and MS launches a marine investigator to the scene as appropriate to gather sufficient factual information to develop a marine accident brief. The majority of these brief investigation reports are adopted by MS director approval through delegated authority.

MS is also responsible for overall management of the NTSB international marine safety program, under which we investigate major marine casualties involving foreign-flagged vessels in US territorial waters and US-flagged vessels involved in major marine casualties anywhere in the world. Accidents involving foreign-flagged vessels have accounted for about 30 percent of NTSB marine accident investigations in the past 5 years. Every year, more than 10 million US passengers are carried aboard foreign-flagged cruise ships. MS also participates with the USCG in investigating serious marine casualties involving foreign-flagged vessels in international waters; these include, for example, casualties involving foreign-flagged cruise ships. The international program involves reviewing US position papers related to marine accident investigations and participating in select International Maritime Organization (IMO) meetings.

Under the MS international program, the NTSB also coordinates with other US and foreign agencies to ensure consistency with IMO conventions, most notably in joint US-flag state marine accident investigations. Further, we cooperate with other accident investigation organizations worldwide, such as the Marine Accident Investigators' International Forum; and we track developments in marine accident investigation and prevention worldwide. In the last year, the NTSB participated in IMO meetings on review and classification of maritime accidents and accident reporting, certification and training of mariners, and technical standards and requirements for voyage data recorders.

MS is organized into the Major Investigations Division and the Product Development Division.

Office of Railroad, Pipeline, and Hazardous Materials Investigations (RPH): RPH investigates and evaluates the emergency response to accidents involving railroads, pipelines, and hazardous materials. On the basis of the investigations conducted by this office, the NTSB may issue safety recommendations to federal and state regulatory agencies, industry and safety standards organizations, carriers and pipeline operators, equipment and container manufacturers, producers and shippers of hazardous materials, and emergency response organizations. RPH consists of four divisions: Railroad, Pipeline and Hazardous Materials, Human Performance and Survival Factors, and Report Development.

Office of Research and Engineering (RE): RE provides technical support to NTSB accident investigations in all modes of transportation. The office—consisting of four divisions and one program area—also conducts safety studies, generates periodic statistical reviews of aviation accidents, and provides medical and toxicology support for investigations in all modes. RE comprises the following divisions: Safety Studies and Statistical Analysis, Vehicle Performance, Vehicle Recorders, and Materials Laboratory.

Office of Communications (OC): OC's mission is to ensure that the NTSB's vision and actions are accurately and effectively communicated to congressional stakeholders, victims of transportation accidents and their families, state and local governments, the press, and the public.

The desired result is a clear understanding of the NTSB mission and how implementation of NTSB recommendations addresses critical transportation safety issues. OC staff produces and updates information for the agency's website and creates videos to support the agency's advocacy efforts. OC includes four divisions: Safety Advocacy, Public Affairs, Government Affairs, and Transportation Disaster Assistance.

Safety recommendations are issued to government agencies at all levels, transportation operators, safety organizations, and other key stakeholders to improve the nation's transportation system. The adoption of NTSB safety recommendations is not mandatory, but to emphasize their importance Congress requires the DOT and its agencies to respond to recommendations within 90 days of their issuance.

The OC develops and administers the NTSB's Most Wanted List (MWL) based, in part, on open safety recommendations. The MWL is the agency's preeminent advocacy tool, highlighting issue areas whose resolution would have significant impact on transportation safety at the national and state levels. Although the NTSB actively advocates for the acceptance of all its safety recommendations, follow-up efforts for the recommendations supporting MWL issue areas are generally more aggressive.

Office of Administration (AD): AD coordinates and manages the infrastructure and support activities of the agency. This office provides assistance in the areas of human resource management, labor relations, facilities management, safety, security, acquisitions, and lease management. Physical inventory, shipping and receiving, telecommunications, and management of the NTSB's conference center are also major functions managed by AD. Work is carried out by four divisions: Administrative Operations and Security, Human Resources, Acquisition and Lease Management, and Safety.

Office of Administrative Law Judges (ALJ): The NTSB serves as the "court of appeals" for airmen, mechanics, or mariners whenever the Federal Aviation Administration (FAA) or the USCG takes a certificate action. The NTSB currently has four judges: three are assigned to headquarters in Washington, DC, and one is assigned to the Denver, Colorado, office. They hold hearings based on their circuit assignment.

The agency's administrative law judges hear, consider, and issue initial decisions on administrative appeals regarding FAA aviation enforcement actions. The judges also adjudicate claims for fees and expenses stemming from FAA certificate and civil penalty actions under the Equal Access to Justice Act. The certificate holder or the FAA may appeal the judges' decisions in these cases to the five-member Board. The Board's review on appeal of an administrative law judges' decisions is based on the record of the proceeding, which includes hearing testimony (transcript), exhibits, the judge's decision, and appeal briefs submitted by the parties.

Marine certificate actions are heard first by the USCG administrative law judges and may be appealed to the USCG Commandant. The ruling of the Commandant may then be appealed to the NTSB. The same appellate process is followed for marine certificate actions as is conducted for aviation actions.

Office of the Chief Information Officer (CIO): The CIO provides strategic direction and operational support for NTSB information systems, and develops and distributes programs and products for use by the agency and the public. The CIO consists of four divisions and one program area: Computer Services, Systems Support, Records Management, Enterprise Architecture, and the Information Technology Security Program.

Office of Equal Employment Opportunity, Diversity, and Inclusion (EEODI): The EEODI advises and assists the Chairman and NTSB office directors in carrying out their responsibilities relative to Title VII of the Civil Rights Act of 1964, as amended, and other laws, executive orders, and regulatory guidelines affecting diversity development and Equal Employment Opportunity (EEO) complaints. These services are provided to managers, employees, and job applicants by the EEODI Director and one full-time staff person, three collateral-duty employees (that is, one Hispanic employment program manager, one federal women's program manager, and one disability program manager), and volunteer special emphasis program managers. To maintain the integrity and impartiality of the NTSB EEO complaints resolution program, external EEO counselors and investigators are contracted to assist employees and job applicants who file informal/formal complaints of alleged discrimination. EEODI services also include the delivery and execution of mandatory on-line and on-site educational training activities, diversity awareness and targeted outreach, and internal recruitment initiatives/career enhancement advisory services, which have resulted in a greater percentage of women and minorities being included in the NTSB workforce. Additionally, the EEODI office manages an alternative dispute resolution program that provides options for resolving EEO disputes at the earliest possible stage.

Office of the Chief Financial Officer (CFO): The CFO manages NTSB financial resources, develops the agency's budget requests for submission to the Office of Management and Budget and Congress, and executes the budget for resources appropriated to the NTSB by Congress. The CFO also prepares the agency's financial statements, as required by the Accountability of Tax Dollars Act; oversees property and inventory control programs; and analyzes the fee structure for services that the agency provides on a reimbursable basis. Additionally, the CFO is responsible for ensuring compliance with the Federal Managers' Financial Integrity Act. The CFO consists of the Budget and Accounting Divisions.

Office of the General Counsel (GC): The GC provides advice and assistance on legal aspects of policy matters, legislation, testimony, NTSB rules, and ethics. The office also provides timely and objective review of airman appeals of certificate actions and certain civil penalties and seaman license actions, acting on behalf of the NTSB on particular procedural aspects of enforcement cases; makes decisions as to the release of official information pursuant to the requests or demands of private litigants, courts, or other authorities for use in litigation not involving the United States; ensures compliance with statutes concerning public access to information through publication of NTSB decisions and releases under the Freedom of Information Act (FOIA); provides counsel and staff assistance to the US Department of Justice when the NTSB is a party to judicial proceedings; and provides internal legal assistance and guidance regarding accident and incident investigations, hearings, appearances as witnesses, acquiring evidence by subpoena and other means, and the taking of depositions.

Office of the Managing Director (MD): The MD assists the Chairman in the discharge of executive and administrative functions. The office coordinates activities of the entire staff, is responsible for day-to-day operation of the agency, and recommends and develops plans to achieve program objectives. The Managing Director is responsible for the overall leadership, direction, and performance of the agency, as well as its communications and organizational efficiency, including management oversight of the NTSB Communications Center. The center provides support 24 hours a day, 7 days a week, year-round, for agency-wide operational requirements, including accident launches and the collection and dissemination of information related to transportation accidents and incidents.

There are two organizational units within the Office of the Managing Director—the Training Center and the Safety Recommendations and Quality Assurance Division. The Training Center manages workforce development and external training functions. The Safety Recommendations and Quality Assurance Division manages safety recommendations and policies concerning document development and review, quality control for NTSB documents and product databases, and the archiving of internal and external correspondence.

Management's Discussion & Analysis

Overview

Since its creation in 1967 as an accident investigation agency within the newly created US Department of Transportation (DOT), the National Transportation Safety Board's (NTSB's) mission has been to determine the probable cause of transportation accidents and incidents and to formulate safety recommendations to improve transportation safety. The NTSB's authority currently extends to the following types of accidents:

- All US civil aviation accidents and certain public aircraft accidents

- Selected highway accidents

- Railroad accidents involving passenger trains or selected freight train accidents that result in fatalities or significant property damage

- Major marine accidents and any marine accident involving both a public and a nonpublic vessel

- Pipeline accidents involving fatalities, substantial property damage, or significant environmental damage

- Selected accidents resulting in the release of hazardous materials in any mode of transportation

- Selected transportation accidents that involve problems of a recurring nature or that are catastrophic

In 1974, Congress passed the Independent Safety Board Act, which severed the NTSB's ties to the DOT and authorized the agency to take the following additional actions:

- Evaluate the effectiveness of government agencies involved in transportation safety

- Evaluate the safeguards used in the transportation of hazardous materials

- Evaluate the effectiveness of emergency responses to hazardous material accidents

- Conduct special studies on safety problems

- Maintain official US census of aviation accidents and incidents

- Review appeals from airmen, mechanics, and repairmen who have been assessed civil penalties by the Federal Aviation Administration (FAA)

- Review appeals from airmen and merchant seamen whose certificates have been revoked or suspended by the US Coast Guard (USCG)

History and Structure of the NTSB

The NTSB opened its doors on April 1, 1967, initially relying on the DOT for funding and administrative support. Although its charter is the Independent Safety Board Act of 1974, the origins of the NTSB can be found in the Air Commerce Act of 1926, in which Congress charged the Commerce Department with investigating the causes of aircraft accidents. The rules of the NTSB are located in Chapter VIII, Title 49 of the CFR.

The NTSB has five Board Members, each nominated by the President and confirmed by the Senate to serve 5-year terms. One Member is designated by the President as Chairman and another as Vice Chairman for 2-year terms. The chairmanship requires separate Senate confirmation. When there is no designated Chairman, the Vice Chairman serves as Acting Chairman.

The Office of the Managing Director assists the Chairman in the discharge of the Chairman's functions as executive and administrative head of the NTSB. The office provides overall leadership for the management of the agency, including production, strategy, and support functions. The office ensures that NTSB resources are allocated appropriately to enable the agency to perform its mission in the most cost-effective manner.

The NTSB's headquarters office is located in Washington, DC. The NTSB also has investigators strategically located in Ashburn, Virginia; Denver, Colorado; Anchorage, Alaska; and Seattle, Washington. The Office of Aviation Safety has organized the staff assigned in the 48 contiguous states into three mega-regional offices; Alaska forms a fourth region. In addition, two aviation investigators are based in Hawaii. The following chart depicts the major organizational components, reporting relationships, and budget program structure of the NTSB.

National Transportation Safety Board
Organization and Program Structure

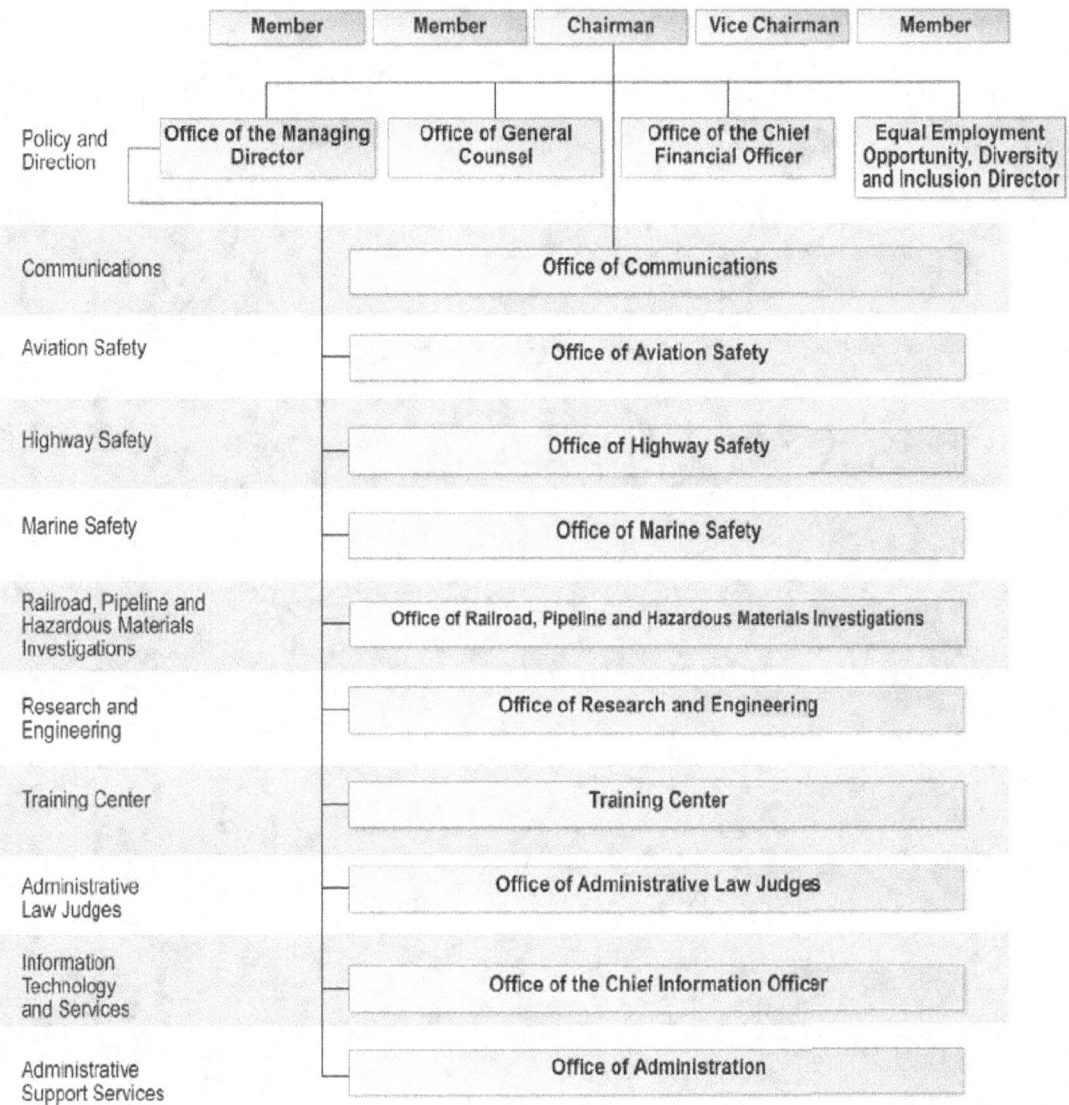

The NTSB Chairman serves as the agency's chief executive and administrative officer. The Board Members, in conjunction with the Chairman, establish policies on transportation safety issues; review and approve major accident reports, safety studies, and safety recommendations; and decide appeals of the initial decisions of the NTSB administrative law judges regarding FAA and USCG certificate actions. They also preside over accident or other transportation safety hearings, testify before congressional committees, and participate in agency go-teams on major investigations.

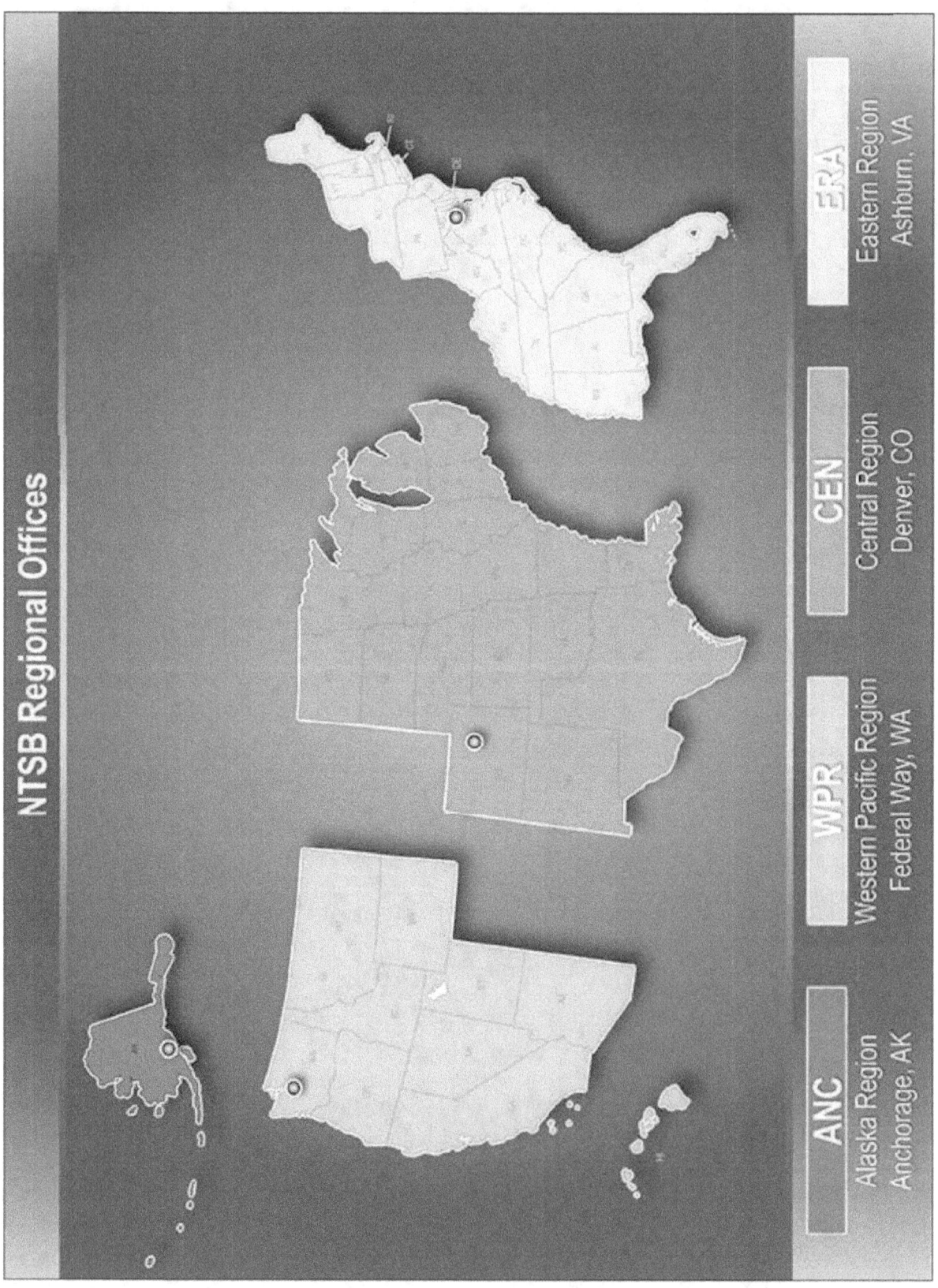

Mission

As discussed in previous sections, the NTSB is an independent federal agency dedicated to promoting aviation, railroad, highway, marine, pipeline, and hazardous materials safety. Established in 1967, the agency is mandated by Congress through the Independent Safety Board Act of 1974 to investigate transportation accidents, determine the probable causes of the accidents, issue safety recommendations, study transportation safety issues, and evaluate the safety effectiveness of government agencies involved in transportation. The NTSB makes public its actions and decisions through accident reports, safety studies, special investigation reports, safety recommendations, and statistical reviews.

Independence

The NTSB's status as an independent government agency makes it different from other stakeholders in the transportation industry. Transportation companies are motivated by financial gain, and many are ultimately accountable to their shareholders. Other government agencies (for example, the FAA, the Federal Railroad Administration, the Federal Highway Administration, and the USCG) have an official role in establishing and enforcing industry regulations. The NTSB has no such interests or obligations. Our most important stakeholder is the traveling public, and we are concerned with one thing: *promoting transportation safety for the traveling public.*

Investigations

NTSB staff take an unbiased approach to each accident that the agency investigates. Local authorities, industry representatives, and other agencies are frequently called upon to participate as parties to the NTSB's investigations. Our only objectives are to determine the probable cause of the accident and to extract lessons learned that will prevent similar accidents in the future. The NTSB's reputation as an honest broker is a key reason why state and local governments, federal agencies, and even foreign countries welcome and encourage the NTSB to lead important accident investigations.

Actions to correct deficiencies that contribute to accidents are often identified early in the investigative process. The NTSB strongly supports and encourages voluntary efforts to effect safety changes and works with parties to implement such changes. In other situations, the NTSB invokes the more formal process of issuing safety recommendations, which ask government agencies, parties to the investigation, or other entities to take action to improve safety. Some of these recommendations are issued during the accident investigation. In other cases, the NTSB makes safety recommendations at the conclusion of the investigative process and incorporates them into the official accident reports.

Performance

Strategic Goals, Objectives, Strategies, and Performance Measures

Strategic Goal No. 1: Conduct Effective Accident Investigations

Summary

Strategic goal no. 1 focuses on the NTSB's key challenges of identifying those accidents in each transportation mode that represent the most important targets of investigative opportunity, determining the scope and scale of such investigations, and conducting safety studies to help to prevent similar accidents in the future.

Our status as an independent federal agency sets us apart from other stakeholders in the transportation industry. Our most important stakeholder is the traveling public, and we are concerned with one principal objective: promoting transportation safety. Conducting independent accident investigations is a critical component of our mission, and it is done with transparency, accountability, and integrity, which are core values of the agency.

The NTSB is obligated to participate in aviation investigations in foreign countries when they involve US carriers or US-manufactured or -designed equipment. This effort helps ensure that USbuilt or -designed aircraft do not have safety issues. Our participation in foreign aviation investigations has led to improvements in aviation safety here and abroad. NTSB-led domestic investigations have also benefitted from the participation of other international accident investigation agencies. Our role in international activities for all modes of transportation includes unique challenges, but with our continued advocacy and outreach, we can showcase lessons learned and improve awareness of these investigations nationally and internationally.

Accomplishing strategic goal no. 1 will ensure effective and efficient investigation of accidents and incidents and foster a transportation industry that is better prepared to address safety issues.

The NTSB applies the following objectives, strategies, and performance measures to achieve this goal:

Objectives

- Select and scale appropriate responses to accident investigations and incidents.
- Increase recognition of the NTSB role in investigating international aviation accidents.
- Continue to effectively coordinate and deliver transportation disaster assistance (TDA) to the families of accident victims.
- Engage in outreach with the transportation community to improve awareness of lessons learned from accident investigations nationally and internationally.

Strategies

- Revise and periodically review selection criteria and other tools as necessary to improve and to expedite investigations.

- Continue to advance our role in international aviation accidents and to participate in aviation investigations in foreign countries.

- Improve our capacity to conduct safety studies.

- Develop outreach plans and products such as videos and digests based on investigations and studies.

- Assist investigators in all modes of transportation by interacting with accident victims and family members.

Performance Measures

- Number of products adopted by the Board.

- Average time (in months) to complete Board-adopted products.

- Number of cooperative activities in international aviation completed.

- Percent of TDA support provided to major aviation and rail accident investigations, as legislated.

- Number of outcome-oriented safety results (legislation, federal rules, industry symposiums, or lessons learned) involving industry or government stakeholders following outreach efforts.

Key Management Issues and Challenges

The cost of transportation accidents to society is significant, and the growth in transportation system activity in the United States will intensify the problem. Accompanying this growth are enormous increases in the system's complexity, which must be addressed with techniques and methods of accident investigation that are equally complex. A key challenge for the NTSB is to identify those accidents in each transportation mode that represent the most important targets of investigative opportunity and to determine the appropriate scope and scale of such investigations. This selection process must balance the significance of the safety issues involved against the limited investigative resources available to the NTSB and the depth of the investigation required to develop the safety issues.

To conduct thorough accident investigations, NTSB investigators must stay abreast of the latest technology in the transportation industry; this requires substantial and continuing training. The NTSB is challenged to identify the available resources and staff to provide training in these areas and schedule timely and appropriate training, working around the number and timing of accidents and the limited number of NTSB investigators. The number of major airline accidents worldwide has increased, and NTSB aviation safety staff participate in 19 major foreign accident investigations annually, on average. This level of international participation presents a particular challenge because the office must also continue to meet its mandate to investigate all aviation accidents in the United States.

Strategic Goal No. 2: Recommend and Advocate Actions to Improve Global Transportation Safety

Summary

Because our mission is to be a premier organization improving transportation safety, strategic goal no. 2, which affects the safety of the entire transportation system, cascades into strategic objectives that emphasize advocacy and outreach. Issuing, advancing, and closing safety recommendations are key NTSB functions. This goal also emphasizes our need to promote items on the Most Wanted List. The Most Wanted List is designed as a transparent tool to increase awareness of, and support for, the most critical changes needed to reduce transportation accidents and save lives. Leveraging our unique position in the safety industry, we believe it is necessary to lead the transportation community with integrity to ensure that emerging safety issues are being addressed and that political leadership is aware of public policy implications.

To achieve this goal, the NTSB applies the following objectives, strategies, and measures:

Objectives

- Identify new and creative ways to advocate safety recommendations and other safety actions.
- Maintain and advocate items on the Most Wanted List.

Strategies

- Implement appropriate safety recommendations from investigations and safety studies.
- Publicly recognize safety recommendations that are implemented and those that, being unimplemented, result in persistent risk.
- Publicize the up-to-date status of all safety recommendations through the NTSB website and other public communication channels.
- Increase advocacy efforts on emerging safety issues through ongoing dialogue with relevant government and other stakeholders, testimony, and other public communications.

Performance Measures

- Number of safety recommendations adopted over the last 5 years.
- Percent of Most Wanted List issue areas that are new to the list.

Key Management Issues and Challenges

The nation's level of transportation activity, which highly correlates with its economic activity, continues to increase. As our skies, highways, waterways, and railways become more congested, the potential for transportation accidents increases. With limited resources, the NTSB is challenged to identify ways to achieve implementation of its open safety recommendations. Another concern is how to increase the NTSB presence at state legislative sessions to elevate the priority of highway safety at the state level and advance legislators' understanding of the issues.

Finally, because of the length and complexity of the rulemaking process, federal agencies are frequently not implementing NTSB recommendations in a timely fashion. The NTSB is challenged to ensure that the rulemaking process, which can take years, does not hamper the successful implementation of recommendations. Working with Congress, other government agencies, and industry groups, the NTSB takes an active role in leading efforts for a safer transportation system. During FY 2014, the NTSB adopted 62 products. The Board conducted 42 outreach efforts to advance transportation safety among industry and government stakeholders, which led to important safety results. Over the last five years, implementation of NTSB safety recommendations in all modes of transportation increased with 705 recommendations having been implemented.

Strategic Goal No. 3: Conduct Fair and Expeditious Adjudication of Airman and Mariner Appeals from the FAA and the USCG Enforcement Actions and Certificate Denials

Summary
Strategic goal no. 3 recognizes our continuing commitment to providing a fair appeals process for airmen and mariners to ensure thorough and independent adjudication, while providing due process to those affected and safeguarding the integrity of the aviation and marine safety enforcement system.

To achieve this goal, the NTSB applies the following objective and strategies:

Objective

- Effectively manage the appeals process and appropriately protect the rights of airmen and mariners seeking the NTSB's review, balancing their interests with those of aviation and marine safety.

Strategies

- Continue to increase administrative law judges' case closure rate.
- Continue to decrease non-emergency backlog cases on hand.

Performance Measures

- Percentage of cases disposed of during the fiscal year.
- Number of non-emergency enforcement backlog cases on hand.

Key Management Issues and Challenges
The NTSB serves as the "court of appeals" for airmen and mariners facing the loss or suspension of their licensing certificates or the imposition of a civil penalty. As the level of transportation activity increases, the potential for transportation accidents increases, resulting in more enforcement cases; consequently, effective management of the appeals process becomes more challenging. We will continue to promote transportation safety by adjudicating appeals of certificate actions and denials, providing due process to those affected, and ensuring the integrity of the aviation and maritime safety enforcement system. During FY 2014, the NTSB Office of Administrative Law Judges closed 66 percent of cases received.

Strategic Goal No. 4: Provide Outstanding Mission Support

Summary

Providing mission support in achieving our first three goals is imperative if we are to retain our leadership in influencing changes, increasing transparency and outreach, and advancing transportation safety. Strategic goal no. 4 captures the overall nature of the organization—excellence—and ensures that we are able to fulfill our broad mission.

The strategic objectives for this goal concern maintaining agency resources; improving employee safety and health knowledge, human capital, diversity, and inclusion; and maintaining effective communications. This goal emphasizes the agency's challenge to enhance our management of information and data to ensure reliable and consistent information for management and staff. We remain focused on hiring the right people and on effectively capturing and transferring knowledge. We foster a culture of leadership, diversity, and accountability that enables decisionmaking while promoting teamwork and collaboration. In addition, we strive to meet challenges with innovation and urgency. Collectively, these efforts support our fulfillment of this strategic goal as well as our mission of independently advancing transportation safety.

To achieve this goal, the NTSB applies the following objectives and strategies:

Objectives

- Efficiently utilize and manage agency resources.
- Align and improve human capital planning and diversity.

Strategies

- Provide accurate, timely, and useful financial information to agency managers and staff to support effective decision-making.
- Manage agency information and employ information technology (IT) to improve the productivity, effectiveness, and efficiency of agency programs and to enhance the availability and usefulness of information to all users, both within and outside the agency.
- Continue to improve safety and health training and education to assist the agency in employing sound risk management practices.
- Use innovative strategies to recruit, develop, and retain a high-quality, diverse workforce.
- Create an agency-wide performance culture focused on individual and organizational accountability to achieve the NTSB's programmatic goals and priorities.
- Sustain a learning environment that provides for continuing improvement in performance through knowledge management, performance feedback, training, coaching, and mentoring.
- Continue to foster a work environment that is free from discrimination and provides maximum opportunities for all employees to use their diverse talents in support of the NTSB's mission and goals.
- Continue to identify new and improved methods of communicating internally and externally.

Performance Measures

- Obtain an audit opinion on financial statements to ensure that records are maintained to the highest level of integrity.

- Increase integration of IT solutions into NTSB mission and administrative processes.

- Obtain positive responses to the Federal Information Security Management Act (FISMA), FOIA, and other oversight body reports.

- Implement the NTSB Safety and Occupational Health Program.

- Develop and implement a Strategic Hiring Plan.

- Increase the number of formal and informal development programs/events.

- Implement diversity and inclusion organizational development activities.

Key Management Issues and Challenges

The NTSB has earned a reputation for thorough and independent investigation of transportation accidents. To maintain that reputation, we are committed to continuing to develop the managerial, leadership, and workforce skills needed to ensure the quality of the accident investigations for which we are well known. This initiative includes the entire NTSB organization—investigative offices, business support offices, and agency leadership. We are faced with the challenge of developing our workforce in an environment of technological changes and dwindling resources.

This challenge is addressed by effective long-range planning and excellent communications. Long-range planning in human capital management, as well as in core operations, ensures that the NTSB is fully equipped to deal with any future investigative need. The NTSB's enhanced focus on planning results in a workforce and processes that are capable and flexible enough to respond effectively to any and all issues and challenges. Effective communications at all levels of the organization ensure that we continually improve our plans and processes. We will devote time and resources to thinking strategically and developing our staff. To achieve our long-term vision, we must effectively plan and communicate while maintaining our primary commitment to investigating transportation accidents. We believe that the initiatives in place will provide the necessary balance to ensure success with this strategic goal.

Environmental Analysis

The NTSB's ability to achieve our strategic goals may be influenced by the changing balance of industry operations; other federal, state, and local government activities; national priorities; market forces; and resource availability. The following factors may affect the achievement of strategic goals for FYs 2013 to 2016:

- Challenges in achieving closure of significant recommendations.

- Difficulty in retaining and recruiting staff with critical technical experience.

- Dealing with retirement or attrition of key personnel.

- Managing under budgetary constraints, including fluctuations in appropriations.

- Responding to emerging technologies that affect the NTSB's investigative process as well as its advocacy and outreach efforts.

Evaluation and Planning Process

The agency's approach to performance measure evaluation has helped drive its overall planning process. Over the last 3 years, the planning process has been improved by streamlined collection and reporting techniques. Overall, the agency has improved the selection and evaluation of performance measures, resulting in measures that have been designated as priorities for the agency and can be accomplished in 2 years or less. The measures are more aligned with our strategic objectives in our strategic and annual operating plans. This approach will continue into the future and will result in additional improvements to the evaluation of our planning process.

Improper Payments Elimination and Recovery Act (IPERA) Compliance

Only a small portion of the NTSB budget is subject to IPERA reporting. The vast majority of NTSB payments are to employees in the form of payroll and travel reimbursement, as well as intragovernmental payments, such as those made to the Interior Business Center (IBC) for financial services and to the US General Services Administration for rent. Payments subject to the IPERA are primarily vendor payments.

For FY 2014, we made approximately 2,627 vendor payments totaling about $17 million. For FY 2013, we made approximately 2,973 vendor payments totaling about $19 million. The NTSB is committed to minimizing the risk of improper payments. We use a variety of system controls, separation of duties, and other procedures to reduce that risk and to promptly identify any improper payments that might occur. These controls are tested as part of the SSAE 16, A-123, and financial statement audit processes; they are also considered during the annual FMFIA process.

Given these controls, we estimate the improper payments rate to be less than 0.01 percent and the improper payments amount to be $1,700 or less. This level is below the threshold established by the OMB and therefore does not represent significant improper payments. Accordingly, no plan is proposed to further reduce improper payments nor would a recovery audit program be cost effective.

Financial Statements

A Message from the Chief Financial Officer

It is my pleasure to report that during FY 2014, the NTSB continued to honor its commitment to lead by example in government financial management. For the twelfth consecutive year, since being required to prepare audited financial statements, our independent auditors presented the NTSB with an unmodified (clean) opinion on our financial statements.

The financial statements that follow were prepared, audited, and made publicly available as an integral part of this performance and accountability report (PAR). These financial statements fairly present the NTSB's financial position and were prepared in accordance with generally accepted accounting principles in the United States of America and of the Office of Management and Budget.

In FY 2014, the NTSB continued its efforts toward organizational excellence, which is defined by results. Progress for much of our efforts toward excellence is captured in the NTSB FY 2014 and 2013 PAR. The report provides the NTSB's most important financial and performance information. It is also our principal publication and report to Congress and the American people on our program leadership and our stewardship and management of the public funds entrusted to us.

Attainment of the independent auditor's unmodified opinion on our financial statement demonstrates the Office of the Chief Financial Officer's commitment to moving forward vigorously during FY 2014 to continue to improve our internal control processes and fulfill our financial management goals.

Edward Benthall
November 1, 2014

**U.S. Department of
Transportation**
Office of the Secretary
of Transportation

Office of Inspector General
Washington, DC 20590

November 10, 2014

The Honorable Christopher A. Hart
Acting Chairman
National Transportation Safety Board
490 L'Enfant Plaza, SW
Washington, DC 20594

Dear Acting Chairman Hart:

I respectfully submit our report on the quality control review (QCR) of the National Transportation Safety Board's (NTSB) financial statement audit for fiscal years 2014 and 2013.

Leon Snead & Company, P.C. (LSC) of Rockville, MD, completed the audit of NTSB's financial statements as of and for the years ended September 30, 2014, and September 30, 2013 (see Enclosure), under contract to the Office of Inspector General. The contract required LSC to perform the audit in accordance with generally accepted Government auditing standards and Office of Management and Budget (OMB) Bulletin 14-02, "Audit Requirements for Federal Financial Statements."

LSC concluded that the financial statements present fairly, in all material respects, NTSB's financial position, net cost, changes in net position, and budgetary resources, as of and for the years ended September 30, 2014, and September 30, 2013, in conformity with U.S. generally accepted accounting principles.

LSC's Fiscal Year 2014 Audit Report

LSC reported one significant deficiency in internal control over financial reporting. The report did not include any instances of reportable noncompliance with laws and regulations tested.

Significant Deficiency

Internal Control Weaknesses Impacted Interim Financial Statements - NTSB took actions to address the material internal control weakness over financial reporting cited in its fiscal year 2013 financial statement audit.[1] However, LSC identified errors with two journal vouchers that the Agency processed, and compilation and presentation errors in NTSB's interim financial statements as of June 30, 2014. As a result, the interim financial statements that NTSB provided to OMB and for the financial statement audit contained misstatements. These problems were primarily attributed to the fact that personnel in the Office of Chief Financial Officer need to consistently follow established controls over the preparation, review and approval of journal vouchers, and over the financial statements' compilation and presentation. NTSB subsequently took corrective action. As a result, the year-end financial statements were fairly stated in all material respects.

We performed a QCR of LSC's report and related documentation. Our QCR, as differentiated from an audit performed in accordance with generally accepted Government auditing standards, was not intended for us to express, and we do not express an opinion on NTSB's financial statements or conclusions about the effectiveness of internal controls or compliance with laws and regulations. LSC is responsible for its report dated November 6, 2014, and the conclusions expressed in that report. However, our QCR disclosed no instances in which LSC did not comply, in all material respects, with generally accepted Government auditing standards.

LSC made one recommendation to strengthen NTSB's financial reporting controls. We agree with this recommendation and are not making any additional recommendations. NTSB concurred with the significant deficiency, agreed with the recommendation, and committed to continue implementing corrective actions.

---

[1] In fiscal year 2013, LSC reported a material weakness in financial reporting due to the compilation and preparation of the interim financial statements, and posting model errors that impacted the financial statements. NTSB experienced problems in converting to a new accounting system through its service provider in fiscal year 2013, thereby compounding the issues identified.

We appreciate the cooperation and assistance of NTSB's representatives and LSC. If you have any questions, please call me at (202) 366-1407, or George Banks, Program Director, at (410) 962-1729.

Sincerely,

Louis C. King
Assistant Inspector General for Financial and
    Information Technology Audits

Enclosure

LEON SNEAD
& COMPANY, P.C.

Certified Public Accountants
& Management Consultants

416 Hungerford Drive, Suite 400
R ckville, Maryland 20850
301-738-8190
Fax: 301-738-8210
le snead companypc@erols.com

Independent Auditor's Report

Inspector General, Department of Transportation
Chairman, National Transportation Safety Board

We have a dited the accompanying b lance sheet of National Transportation Safety Board
(NTSB) as of September 30, 2014 and 2013, and the related statements of net cost, statements of
changes i net pos ion, and s tements of budgetary resources (financial statemen s) for the
years then ended. The objective of our audit was to express an opinion on the fair presentation
of these financial statements. In connection with our audit, we also considered the NTSB's
internal control over financial reporting and tested the NTSB's compliance with certain
provisions of applicable laws, regulations, and contracts that could have a direct and material
effect on these financial statements.

SUMMARY

As stated in our opinion on the financial statements, we found that the NTSB's financial
statements, as of and for the years ended September 30, 2014 and 2013, are presented fairly, in
all material respects, in conformity with accounting principles generally accepted in the United
States of America.

Our consideration of internal control would not necessarily disclose all deficiencies in internal
control over financial reporting that might be material weaknesses under standards issued by the
American Institute of Certified Public Accountants. However, our testing of internal control
identified a significant deficiency in internal controls over financial reporting. Specifically, we
found that controls over the processing of journal vouchers (JV), and the compilation and
preparation of the interim financial statements, were not always followed.

As a result of our tests of compliance with certain provisions of laws regulations, and significant
provisions of contracts nothing came to our attention that caused us to believe that NTSB failed
to comply with applicable laws regulations, or significant provisions of contracts that have a
material effect on the financial statements insofar as they relate to accounting matters.

The following sections discuss in more detail our opinion on the NTSB's financial statements,
our consideration of the NTSB's internal control over financial reporting, our tests of NTSB's
compliance with certain provisions of applicable laws and regulations, and management's and
our responsibilities.

REPORT ON THE FINANCIAL STATEMENTS

We have audited the accompanying financial statements of NTSB, which comprise the balance sheets as of September 30, 2014 and 2013, and the related statements of net cost, changes in net position, and budgetary resources for the years then ended, and the related notes to the financial statements.

Management's Responsibility for the Financial Statements

Management is responsible for the preparation and fair presentation of these financial statements in accordance with accounting principles generally accepted in the United States of America. Such responsibility includes the design, implementation, and maintenance of internal control relevant to the preparation and fair presentation of financial statements that are free from material misstatement, whether due to error or fraud.

Auditor's Responsibility

Our responsibility is to express an opinion on these financial statements based on our audits. We conducted our audits in accordance with auditing standards generally accepted in the United States of America; standards applicable to financial statement audits contained in *Government Auditing Standards*, issued by the Comptroller General of the United States of America; and OMB Bulletin 14-02, *Audit Requirements for Federal Financial Statements* (the OMB audit bulletin). Those standards and the OMB audit bulletin require that we plan and perform the audit to obtain reasonable assurance about whether the financial statements are free from material misstatement.

An audit involves performing procedures to obtain audit evidence about the amounts and disclosures in the financial statements. The procedures selected depend on the auditor's judgment, including the assessment of the risks of material misstatement of the financial statements, whether due to fraud or error. In making those risk assessments in a Federal agency, the auditor considers internal control relevant to the entity's preparation and fair presentation of the financial statements in order to design audit procedures that are appropriate in the circumstances, but not for the purpose of expressing opinions on the effectiveness of the NTSB's internal control or its compliance with laws, regulations, and significant provisions of contracts. Accordingly, no opinion is expressed. An audit also includes evaluating the appropriateness of accounting policies used and the reasonableness of significant accounting estimates made by management, as well as evaluating the overall presentation of the financial statements.

We believe that the audit evidence we have obtained is sufficient and appropriate to provide a basis for our audit opinion.

Opinion

In our opinion, the financial statements referred to above present fairly, in all material respects, the financial position of NTSB as of September 30, 2014 and 2013, and the related net cost, changes in net position, and budgetary resources for the years then ended in accordance with accounting principles generally accepted in the United States of America.

OTHER MATTERS

Required Supplementary Information

Accounting principles generally accepted in the U.S. require that Management's Discussion and Analysis be presented to supplement the basic financial statements. Such information, although not a part of the basic financial statements, is required by the Federal Accounting Standards Advisory Board (FASAB) who considers it to be an essential part of financial reporting for placing the basic financial statements in an appropriate operational, economic, or historical context. We have applied certain limited procedures to the required supplementary information in accordance with auditing standards generally accepted in the United States of America. This consisted of inquiries of management about the methods of preparing the information and comparing the information for consistency with management's responses to our inquiries, the financial statements, and other knowledge we obtained during our audit of the financial statements. We do not express an opinion or provide any assurance on the information because the limited procedures do not provide us with sufficient evidence to express an opinion or provide any assurance.

Other Information

Our audit was conducted for the purpose of forming an opinion on the basic financial statements taken as a whole. The performance measures and other accompanying information are presented for the purposes of additional analysis and are not required parts of the basic financial statements. Such information has not been subjected to the auditing procedures applied in the audit of the basic financial statements, and accordingly, we do not express an opinion or provide any assurance on it.

OTHER AUDITOR REPORTING REQUIREMENTS

Report on Internal Control

In planning and performing our audit of the financial statements of NTSB as of and for the years ended September 30, 2014 and 2013, in accordance with auditing standards generally accepted in the United States of America, we considered the NTSB's internal control over financial reporting (internal control) as a basis for designing audit procedures that are appropriate in the circumstances for the purpose of expressing our opinion on the financial statements, but not for the purpose of expressing an opinion on the effectiveness of the NTSB's internal control. Accordingly, we do not express an opinion on the effectiveness of the NTSB's internal control.

Our consideration of internal control was for the limited purpose described in the preceding paragraph and was not designed to identify all deficiencies in internal control that might be material weaknesses or significant deficiencies and; therefore, material weaknesses or significant deficiencies may exist that were not identified. However, as discussed below, we identified certain deficiencies in internal control that we consider to be a significant deficiency.

Because of inherent limitations in internal controls, including the possibility of management override of controls, misstatements, losses, or noncompliance may nevertheless occur and not be detected. A deficiency in internal control exists when the design or operation of a control does not allow management or employees, in the normal course of performing their assigned functions, to prevent, or detect and correct, misstatements on a timely basis. A material weakness is a deficiency or a combination of deficiencies, in internal control, such that there is a reasonable possibility that a material misstatement of the entity's financial statements will not be prevented, or detected and corrected, on a timely basis. A significant deficiency is a deficiency, or a combination of deficiencies, in internal control that is less severe than a material weakness, yet important enough to merit attention by those charged with governance.

FINDINGS AND RECOMMENDATIONS

Internal Control Weaknesses Impacted Interim Financial Statements

Although the National Transportation Safety Board (NTSB) took actions to address the material internal control weakness over financial reporting as reported in our fiscal year (FY) 2013 financial statement audit, we identified errors with two journal vouchers (JVs) processed by the agency, and compilation and presentation errors in the June 30, 2014, interim financial statements. We attributed the problems noted, primarily, to the need for Office of Chief Financial Officer (OCFO) personnel to more effectively implement established controls over the preparation, review and approval of JVs; and the compilation and presentation of the financial statements. As a result, misstatements were included in the June 30, 2014, interim financial statements provided to OMB and for audit.

Office of Management and Budget (OMB) Circular A-136, *Financial Reporting Requirements,* OMB Circular A-123, *Management's Responsibility for Internal Control,* and applicable NTSB Chief Financial Officer (CFO) operating policies, as published on the NTSB internal website, provide the guidance on financial statement presentation and related areas, and internal controls.

The Government Accountability Office's (GAO), "Standards for Internal Control in the Federal Government," provides that internal control and all transactions and other significant events need to be clearly documented, and the documentation should be readily available for examination. The GAO standards further provide that the documentation requirement should appear in management directives, administrative policies, or operating manuals, and further states that "Internal control should generally be designed to assure that ongoing monitoring occurs in the course of normal operations. It is performed continually and is ingrained in the agency's operations. It includes regular management and supervisory activities, comparisons, reconciliations, and other actions people take in performing their duties."

OMB Circular A-136, Financial Reporting Requirements, Section II.4.1 provides that reporting entities should ensure that information in the financial statements is presented in accordance with GAAP for Federal entities and the requirements of the Circular.

Journal Voucher Controls

a. Control processes for critical documents such as JVs must be in place and operating effectively, or the risk of misstatements increases significantly. JVs bypass accounting and reporting edits built into the accounting system, and may bypass U.S. Treasury approved U.S. Standard General Ledger (USSGL) posting models, allowing any entry (that balances) to be posted to the general ledger. Therefore, controls over JVs should ensure that documentation clearly supports the need for the JV and the entries proposed, and the JV and supporting documentation are thoroughly reviewed and approved by supervisory personnel.

From October 1, 2014, through June 30, the NTSB processed approximately 80 JVs to post accruals, correct postings, and to post other budgetary and proprietary accounting events. We reviewed 57 JVs processed during this period, and found that the controls over this area were properly designed, but not always followed. There were errors with two of the 57 JVs tested. The following table summarizes the problems we found:

JV No.	Amount	Issue	NTSB Corrected
JV 14JUN009	$1,543,772[1] $2,584,676[2]	NTSB erroneously posted a JV to capitalize renovation costs, which had been properly expensed in the prior period (FY 2013) and the current FY, as a leasehold improvement. This impacted the BS, SNC, SCNP, and SBR/SCNP footnote reconciliation in a material amount[3].	Yes
JV 14APR001	$144,381.25	The JV posted anticipated revenue, but was not reversed when the funds were collected. This resulted in an overstatement of Spending Authority from Offsetting Collections and Apportionments on the SBR.	Yes

Because of the significance of a prior period adjustment, we discussed the reasons for JV14JUN009 with OCFO officials, and requested additional information on this JV. For FY 2013 through June 2014, NTSB had accounted for the costs associated with a renovation project as an expense. OCFO officials stated that they initiated a review of the accounting for these costs in the spring of 2014 because of the large costs involved. After review, OCFO personnel determined that the prior handling of the costs was incorrect, and that the costs should have been capitalized as leasehold improvements. Therefore, a JV was prepared by OCFO personnel, reviewed and approved by OCFO supervisory personnel, and posted to the general ledger to reclassify and capitalize about $4.1 million in expenses posted during FY 2013 and 2014.

After we questioned the support for the reclassification and prior period adjustment, OCFO officials initiated another review of this JV, to include the accounting standards and the support for the cost re-classification. As a result, OCFO officials determined that the original accounting for the renovation costs was correct, promptly reversed the prior period adjustment and current year reclassification, and prepared revised June 30, 2014, financial statements and footnotes for audit.

We reviewed relevant accounting standards, and the documentation provided by OCFO officials, and concurred that the original accounting for the renovation costs was correct,

---

[1] Prior Period Adjustment to FY 2013.
[2] FY 2014 adjustment.
[3] Balance Sheet (BS), Statement of Net Cost (SNC). Statement of Changes in Net Position (SCNP). Statement of Budgetary Resources.

and the JV that processed the prior period adjustment and reclassification of FY 2014 expenses was in error and should be reversed.

Our testing of journal vouchers for the period July 1 through September 30, 2014, found that the internal controls over financial reporting were operating effectively, and journal vouchers processed during this period were posted appropriately and supported.

b. Presentation Errors in Interim Financial Statements

Interim financial statements contained errors that should have been detected and corrected prior to submitting the documents to OMB, and for audit. While the number and dollar value of the errors was reduced significantly between our FY 2013 and our FY 2014 interim testing, established controls need to be more effectively implemented to ensure that errors are eliminated from the financial statements. Details follow:

- Presentation errors were made in the Statement of Budgetary Resources (SBR). Our audit found that NTSB incorrectly reported uncollected payments, federal sources, end of year, totaling $512,038, as part of the calculations of unpaid obligations, end of year.

- Presentation errors were made in the SBR when NTSB did not include the line items detailing Budget Authority and Outlays, Net, as required by the OMB Circular A-136.

- Footnote 7, Liabilities Covered and Not Covered by Budgetary Resources, and Footnote 8, Leases, were misstated by $295,000 because of computation errors made when preparing these statements.

These issues were corrected and had no impact on the September 30, 2014, financial statements.

Recommendation

Provide training to applicable OCFO personnel concerning the agency's internal controls over financial reporting to ensure that controls are more effectively implemented over the processing of JVs, and compilation and presentation errors are eliminated.

Report on Compliance

As part of obtaining reasonable assurance about whether the agency's financial statements are free of material misstatement, we performed tests of its compliance with certain provisions of laws, regulations, and significant provisions of contracts, noncompliance with which could have a direct and material effect on the determination of financial statement amounts, and certain other laws and regulations specified in the OMB audit bulletin. We limited our tests of compliance to these provisions and we did not test compliance with all laws and regulations applicable to the NTSB. Providing an opinion on compliance with certain provisions of laws, regulations, and significant contract provisions was not an objective of our audit and, accordingly, we do not express such an opinion.

In connection with our audit, nothing came to our attention that caused us to believe that NTSB failed to comply with applicable laws, regulations, or significant provisions of laws, regulations, and contracts that have a material effect on the financial statements. However, our audit was not directed primarily toward obtaining knowledge of such noncompliance. Accordingly, had we performed additional procedures, other matters may have come to our attention regarding the NTSB's noncompliance with applicable laws, regulations, or significant provisions of laws, regulations, and contracts.

Restricted Use Relating to Reports on Internal Control and Compliance

The purpose of the communication included in the sections identified as "Report on Internal Control" and "Report on Compliance" is solely to describe the scope of our testing of internal control over financial reporting and compliance, and to describe any material weaknesses, significant deficiencies, or instances of noncompliance we noted as a result of that testing. Our objective was not to provide an opinion on the design or effectiveness of the NTSB's internal control over financial reporting or its compliance with laws, regulations, or provisions of contracts. The two sections of the report referred to above are integral parts of an audit performed in accordance with *Government Auditing Standards* in considering the NTSB's internal control over financial reporting and compliance. Accordingly, those sections of the report are not suitable for any other purpose.

Agency Comments and Auditor Evaluation

In commenting on the draft of this report, the Chief Financial Officer advised that the agency concurs with the facts and conclusions in the audit report; the agency has completed actions to address the issues in the report in most areas, and will ensure that all remaining corrective actions are completed timely. A copy of management's response is attached to this report.

Leon Snead & Company, P.C.
Rockville, Maryland
November 6, 2014

Status of Prior Year Recommendations

Rec. No.	Audit Recommendations	Status As of September 30, 2014
1.	Ensure new accounting events are properly researched and recorded.	Closed.
2.	Track identified posting model errors, quantify the impact of the errors, and make necessary adjustments to correct financial statements and budgetary reports.	Closed.
3.	Strengthen internal controls relating to the preparation of the financial statements, and the proper classification of accounts payable and other liabilities.	Closed.
4.	Review the agency's financial statement compilation and presentation operational guidance, and update it periodically to ensure that financial statements are presented in accordance with FASAB and OMB requirements, and address the control issues discussed in this report.	Closed.
5.	Strengthen supervisory reviews of interim and year-end financial statements presented to OMB and for audit, and maintain documentation of these reviews. Ensure that meaningful variance analyses of current and prior year financial statements and footnotes are made and documented.	Open. The portion of the recommendation relating to variance analyses has been closed.

Appendix 2

National Transportation Safety Board
Washington, D.C. 20594

Office of the Chief Financial Officer

DATE: November 6, 2014

TO: Leon Snead
          Partner

FROM: Edward Benthall
          Chief Financial Officer

SUBJECT: DRAFT AUDIT REPORT
          Fiscal Year 2014 and 2013 Financial Statement Audit Report

The National Transportation Safety Board (NTSB) has reviewed the draft fiscal years 2014 and 2013 Financial Statement Audit Report and we concur with the facts and conclusions in the report. We will share the final audit report with senior officials, other interested program managers and staff.

We note that you have agreed that internal controls over financial reporting are no longer a material weakness. There is still work to do in this area as indicated by your recommendations and we will aggressively pursue completion of these actions.

Please convey my appreciation to everyone on your staff who worked diligently on our financial statement audit. If you have any questions or comments, please contact me or Bill Mills at (202) 314-6265.

cc: George Banks, Program Director,
       Financial Audits, DOT OIG

Limitations of the Financial Statements

Responsibility for the integrity and objectivity of the financial information presented in the financial statements lies with NTSB management. The accompanying financial statements report the financial policies and results of the operations of the NTSB, pursuant to the requirements of the United States Code, chapter 31, section 3515(b). Although these financial statements have been prepared from the books and records of the NTSB, they are in addition to the financial reports used to monitor and control budgetary resources, which are prepared from the same books and records. The financial statements should be read with the understanding that the NTSB is an agency of the Executive Branch of the United States Government, a sovereign entity. Accordingly, unfunded liabilities reported in the statements cannot be liquidated without the enactment of an appropriation, and ongoing operations are subjected to enactment of appropriations.

Management Integrity: Controls, Compliance, and Challenges

The NTSB conducts an annual review of the adequacy of the agency's management accountability and controls program in accordance with the FMFIA, revised OMB Circular A 123 "Management's Responsibility for Internal Control".

The NTSB provides reasonable assurance that our programs and resources are protected from waste, fraud, abuse, and mismanagement. This assurance includes certification that the appropriate policies and controls are in place to mitigate the risk of fraud and inappropriate charge card practices. The results of this review are included in the Acting Chairman's Statement of Assurance sent to the President on September 30, 2014. The Acting Chairman's assurance is based on NTSB Office Director Management Control Assurance Memorandums and NTSB responses to Office Directors' Risk Assessments for an Accountability Unit, conducted in accordance with the OMB's guidance in Circular A-123.

The NTSB also relies on the findings and results of audits and studies conducted by the DOT OIG and the Government Accountability Office, other audits and reviews, and the results of our financial statement audit, conducted under the Chief Financial Officers Act of 1990, the Accountability of Tax Dollars Act of 2002, and OMB Circular A-136.

As of September 30, 2014, there are no new material weaknesses to report and the sole prior year weakness has been corrected. The corrected material weakness is NTSB's compliance with "Internal Controls over Financial Reporting."

Discussion and Analysis of Financial Statements

The NTSB's FY 2014 and 2013 financial statements report the agency's financial position and the results of operations on an accrual basis. These annual financial statements comprise a Balance Sheet, a Statement of Net Cost, a Statement of Changes in Net Position, a Statement of Budgetary Resources, and related notes that provide a clear description of the agency and its mission, as well as the significant accounting policies used to develop the statements.

Consolidated Balance Sheet

The major components of the Consolidated Balance Sheet are assets, liabilities, and net position.

Assets. Assets represent agency resources that have future economic benefits. The NTSB's assets totaled $49.2 million in FY 2014. Fund balances with the US Treasury—mostly undisbursed cash balances from appropriated funds—comprised about 73 percent of the total assets. The NTSB does not maintain any cash balances outside of the US Treasury and does not have any revolving or trust funds. Less than one percent of the NTSB's assets were composed of accounts receivable, which reflect funds owed to the NTSB by other federal agencies and the public. The value of equipment, less accumulated depreciation, was $13.0 million.

LIABILITIES. Liabilities are recognized when they are incurred, regardless of whether they are carried by budgetary resources. In FY 2014, the NTSB had total liabilities of $30.7 million. The largest component of these liabilities was a capital lease liability of $13.8 million. Accounts payable reflect funds owed primarily for contracts and other services.

NET POSITION. The NTSB's net position, which reflects the difference between assets and liabilities and represents the agency's financial condition, totals $18.5 million. This amount is broken into two categories: unexpended appropriations (amounts related to undelivered orders and unobligated balances) of $26.7 million and cumulative results of operations (net results of operations since inception plus the cumulative amount of prior period adjustments) of less than $8.2 million. The downward amount in net position was primarily the result of the liabilities not covered by budgetary resources and other liabilities.

Consolidated Statement of Net Cost

The Consolidated Statement of Net Cost represents the net cost to operate the agency. Net costs are composed of gross costs less earned revenues and are reported by the NTSB's major programs. The NTSB's FY 2014 net cost of operations was $102.3 million: $104.2 million in gross costs less $1.9 million in earned revenues.

Consolidated Statement of Changes in Net Position

The Consolidated Statement of Changes in Net Position reports the changes in net position during the reporting period. The NTSB ended FY 2014 with a net position total of $18.5 million. The negative change in net position was primarily the result of the liabilities not covered by budgetary resources and other liabilities.

Combined Statement of Budgetary Resources

The Combined Statement of Budgetary Resources focuses on how budgetary resources (appropriations and reimbursables) were made available, the status of those resources (obligated or unobligated) at the end of the reporting period, and the relationship between the budgetary resources and outlays (collections and disbursements). The NTSB's FY 2014 budgetary resources totaled $121.1 million and primarily consisted of budget authority funds of $102.1 million and an unobligated balance of $19.0 million.

NATIONAL TRANSPORTATION SAFETY BOARD
Balance Sheet
As of September 30, 2014 and 2013

Assets		FY 2014		FY 2013
Intragovernmental:				
Fund balance with Treasury (Note 2)	$	36,210,047	$	34,233,150
Total Intragovernmental Assets	$	36,210,047	$	34,233,150
Accounts receivable (Note 3)	$	14,105	$	434
Property and equipment, net (Note 4)		12,987,236		14,792,968
	$	13,001,341	$	14,793,402
Total Assets	$	**49,211,388**	$	**49,026,552**
Liabilities				
Intragovernmental:				
Accounts payable (Note 7)	$	376,303	$	75,493
Other liabilities (Note 7)		1,593,534		1,583,595
Total Intragovernmental	$	1,969,837	$	1,659,088
Accounts payable (Note 7)	$	1,217,963	$	631,529
Federal Employee Benefits (Note 7)		7,042,672		7,139,580
Capital lease liability (Note 8)		13,829 142		15,088,828
Other Liabilities (Note 7)		6,618,147		6,229,194
Total Liabilities	$	30,677,761	$	30,748,219
Net Position				
Unexpended appropriations	$	26,740,902	$	26,192,015
Cumulative results of operations		(8,207,275)		(7,913,682)
Total Net Position	$	18,533,627	$	18,278,333
Total Liabilities and Net Position	$	**49,211,388**	$	**49,026,552**

NATIONAL TRANSPORTATION SAFETY BOARD
Statement f et Cost
For the Years Ending Sept mber 30, 2014 and 2013

	FY 2014		FY 2013	
	Aviation Safety		**Aviation Safety**	
Gross costs		51,060,730	$	53,897,172
Less: Earned Revenue		(981,600)		(858,010)
Net Costs (Note 9)	$	50,079,130	$	53,039,162
	Surface Transportation Safety		**Surface Transportation Safety**	
Gross costs		30,588,532	$	30,852,363
Less: Earned Revenue		(505,703)		(478,379)
Net Costs (Note 9)	$	30,082,829	$	30,373,984
	Research & Engineering		**Research & Engineering**	
Gross costs		22,552,315	$	21,074,825
Less: Earned Revenue		(380,911)		(312,843)
Net Costs (Note 9)	$	22,171,404	$	20,761,982
Net Cost of Operations (Note 9)	$	**102,333,363**	$	**104,175,128**

NATIONAL TRANSPORTATION SAFETY BOARD
Consolidated Statement of Changes in Net Position
For the Years Ending September 30, 2014 and 2013

	FY 2014 Cumulative Results of Operations	FY 2013 Cumulative Results of Operations
Beginning Balances	($7,913,682)	($8,813,513)
Prior period adjustments (+/-)	-	-
Beginning balances, as adjusted	($7,913,682)	($8,813,513)
Budgetary Financing Sources:		
Appropriations used	$98,337,185	$101,610,516
Other Financing Sources:		
Imputed financing from costs absorbed by others	3,702,585	3,464,443
Total Financing Sources	$102,039,770	$105,074,959
Net Cost of Operations (+/-)	($102,333,363)	($104,175,128)
Net Change	($293,593)	$899,831
Cumulative Results of Operations	($8,207,275)	($7,913,682)

	FY 2014 Unexpended Appropriations	FY 2013 Unexpended Appropriations
Beginning Balances	$26,192,015	$33,189,773
Prior period adjustments (+/-)	-	-
Beginning balances, as adjusted	$26,192,015	$33,189,773
Budgetary Financing Sources:		
Appropriations received	103,027,000	$102,400,000
Other adjustments (rescissions, etc) (+/-)	(4,140,928)	(7,787,242)
Appropriations used	(98,337,185)	(101,610,516)
Total Budgetary Financing Sources	$548,887	($6,997,758)
Total Unexpended Appropriations	$26,740,902	$26,192,015
Net Position	$18,533,627	$18,278,333

NATIONAL TRANSPO TAT ON SAFETY BOARD
Statement of Budgetary Resources
For the Years Ending September 30, 2014 and 2013

	FY 2014	FY 2013
Budgetary Resources		
Unobligated balance brought forward, October 1	16,834,235	18,096,113
Recoveries of prior year obligations	3,413,744	1,857,728
Other changes in unobligated balance	(4,140,928)	(2,431,108)
Unobligated balance from prior year budget authority, net	16,107,051	17,522,733
Appropriations	103,027,000	102,400,000
Permanently not available	-	(5,356,133)
Spending authority from offsetting collections:	2,013,360	1,654,447
Total Budgetary Resources (Note 10)	**121,147,411**	**116,221,047**
Status of Budgetary Resources		
Obligations Incurred (Note 10)	102,134,285	99,386,812
Unobligated balance		
Apportioned	11,577,487	6,983,308
Unapportioned	7,435,639	9,850,927
Total unobligated balance, end of year	19,013,126	16,834,235
Total Budgetary Resources (Note 10)	**121,147,411**	**116,221,047**
Change in Obligated Balances		
Unpaid obligations:		
Unpaid obligations, brought forward, October 1	17,398,915	22,693,542
Obligations Incurred (Note 10)	102,134,285	99,386,812
Gross outlays	(98,909,660)	(102,823,711)
Recoveries of prior year unpaid obligations, net	(3,413,744)	(1,857,728)
Unpaid obligations, end of year	17,209,796	17,398,915
Uncollected payments:		
Uncollected payments from Federal sources	(12,874)	-
Obligated Balance, start of the year	**17,398,915**	**22,693,542**
Obligated Balance, end of year	**17,196,922**	**17,398,915**
Budget Authority and Outlays, net		
Budget Authority, Gross	105,040,360	98,698,314
Actual offsetting collections	(2,000,486)	(1,654,447)
Uncollected payments from Federal sources	(12,874)	-
Budget Authority, Net	**103,027,000**	**97,043,867**
Gross outlays	98,909,660	102,823,711
Actual offsetting collections	(2,000,486)	(1,654,447)
Net Outlays (Note 10)	**96,909,174**	**101,169,264**

Note 1

SUMMARY OF SIGNIFICANT ACCOUNTING POLICIES

Reporting Entity

The accompanying financial statements present the financial position, net cost of operations, changes in net position and budgetary resources of the National Transportation Safety Board (NTSB). The NTSB is an independent federal agency charged with determining the probable cause(s) of transportation accidents and promoting transportation safety. The financial activity presented relates primarily to the execution of the NTSB's congressionally approved budget. The NTSB began operations in 1967 and, although independent, it relied on the U.S. Department of Transportation (DOT) for funding and administrative support. In 1975, under the Independent Safety Board Act, all organizational ties to DOT were severed. The NTSB is not part of DOT, or affiliated with any of its modal agencies. The laws specific to the Board are located in Chapter VIII, Title 49 of the Code of Federal Regulations.

Basis of Accounting and Presentation

These financial statements reflect both accrual and budgetary accounting transactions. Under the accrual method of accounting, revenues are recognized when earned and expenses are recognized as incurred, without regard to receipt or payment of cash. Budgetary accounting is designed to recognize the obligation of funds according to legal requirements. Budgetary accounting is essential for compliance with legal constraints and controls over the use of federal funds.

These financial statements have been prepared from the books and reports of NTSB in accordance with U.S. generally accepted accounting principles (GAAP) for the federal government and the Office of Management and Budget (OMB) Circular A-136.

Assets

Intragovernmental assets are those assets that arise from transactions with other federal entities. Entity assets are available for use by the entity in its operations while nonentity assets are assets held by the entity but not available for use by the entity in its operations.

Fund Balance with U.S. Treasury

The NTSB does not maintain cash in commercial bank accounts. The U.S. Treasury processes cash receipts and disbursements. Funds with the U.S. Treasury consist of appropriated and deposited funds that are available to pay current liabilities and finance authorized purchase commitments.

Accounts Receivable

NTSB's accounts receivable represent amounts due from overpayments to current and non-current employees and from vendors. NTSB maintains an allowance for doubtful accounts for public receivables based on past collection experience. The allowance for doubtful accounts is reviewed and adjusted quarterly.

Property and Equipment

General Property and Equipment

The Office of the Chief Financial Officer has established a capitalization policy for general property and equipment (P&E). General P&E is reported at acquisition cost. The capitalization threshold is established at $25,000. General P&E consists of items that are used by NTSB to support its mission. Depreciation on these assets is calculated using the straight-line method.

The land and buildings in which the NTSB operates are primarily leased from commercial entities. The General Services Administration (GSA) provides some of the facilities occupied by the NTSB. GSA charges the NTSB a Standard Level Users Charge (SLUC) that approximates the commercial rental rates for similar properties.

Leasehold Improvements

The NTSB capitalization policy for leasehold improvements has established a capitalization threshold of $100,000. A leasehold improvement is an improvement of a leased asset that increases the asset's value. Depreciation on these assets is calculated using the straight-line method with ten years as the estimated useful life of the improvements or the remaining term of the lease, whichever is less.

Capital Lease Assets

Any Lease-to-Ownership Plans (LTOP) leases are classified as capital leases. The NTSB has two capital leases. One lease is for space rental on the building that houses the NTSB Ashburn facility. This is a twenty-year lease. Depreciation on the capital lease is calculated using the straight-line method with twenty years, the term of the lease, as the estimated useful life of the capital lease.

The second lease is for copy machines used at all NTSB locations nationwide. This is a five-year lease. Depreciation on the capital lease is calculated using the straight-line method with five years, the term of the lease, as the estimated useful life of the capital lease.

Internal Use Software

The capitalization threshold of internal use software is established at $250,000. Only the costs associated with the software development phase including labor are subject to capitalization. Software development phase activities generally include the design of chosen path, including software configuration and software interfaces, coding, installation to hardware and testing, including the parallel processing phase. Internal use software includes software to operate NTSB programs and software used to produce NTSB goods and services. Depreciation on these assets is calculated using the straight-line method with three years as the estimated useful life of the asset.

Liabilities

Liabilities represent amounts that are likely to be paid by the NTSB as the result of transactions or events that have already occurred; however, no liabilities are paid by the NTSB without an appropriation. Intragovernmental liabilities arise from transactions with other federal entities.

Accounts payable

Accounts payable consist of amounts owed for goods, services and other expenses received but not yet paid.

Accrued Payroll and Benefits

Accrued Payroll and Benefits represents salaries, wages and benefits earned by employees, but not disbursed as of September 30, 2014. Accrued payroll and benefits are payable to employees and are therefore not classified as intragovernmental.

Annual, Sick, and Other Leave

Annual leave is recognized as an expense and as a liability as it is earned; the liability is reduced as leave is taken. Each year, the balance in the accrued annual, restored, and compensatory leave account is adjusted to reflect current leave balances and pay rates. Sick leave and other types of non-vested leave are expensed as taken.

Employee Retirement Plans

Civil Service Retirement System (CSRS) and Federal Employees Retirement System (FERS)
NTSB employees participate in one of two retirement programs, either the CSRS or the FERS, which became effective on January 1, 1987. Most NTSB employees hired after December 31, 1983, are automatically covered by FERS and Social Security.

For CSRS covered employees, the NTSB withheld 7.0 percent of gross earnings. The NTSB matches the withholding, and the sum of the withholding and the matching funds is transferred to the Civil Service Retirement System.

For each fiscal year the Office of Personnel Management (OPM) calculates the U.S. Government's service costs for covered employees, which is an estimate of the amount of funds that, if accumulated annually and invested over an employee's career, would be enough to pay that employee's future benefits. Since the U.S. Government's estimated FY 2014 service cost exceeds contributions made by employer agencies and covered employees, the plan is not fully funded by the NTSB and its employees. As of September 30, 2014, NTSB recognized $3.7 million as an imputed cost and as an imputed financing source for the difference between the estimated service cost and the contributions made by NTSB and its employees.

FERS contributions made by employer agencies and covered employees exceed the U.S. Government's estimated FY 2014 service cost. For FERS covered employees the NTSB made contributions of 11.9 percent of basic pay. Employees contributed .80 percent of gross earnings. Employees participating in FERS are covered under the Federal Insurance Contribution Act (FICA) for which the NTSB contributes a matching amount to the Social Security Administration.

Thrift Savings Plan (TSP)

Employees covered by CSRS and FERS are eligible to contribute to the U.S. Government's TSP, administered by the Federal Retirement Thrift Investment Board. The NTSB makes a mandatory contribution of 1 percent of basic pay for FERS-covered employees. In addition, NTSB makes matching contributions, of up to 5 percent of basic pay, for employees who contribute to the Thrift Savings Plan. Contributions are matched dollar for dollar for the first 3 percent of pay contributed each pay period and 50 cents on the dollar for the next 2 percent of pay. There are no percentage limits on contributions for FERS participants. There are no percentage limits for CSRS participants, but there is no governmental matching contribution. The maximum amounts that either FERS or CSRS employees may contribute to the plan in calendar year 2014 is $17,500. Those age fifty and older may contribute an additional $5,500 in catch up contributions.

The NTSB financial statements do not report CSRS or FERS assets, accumulated plan benefits, or unfunded liabilities, if any, which may be applicable to NTSB employees and funded by NTSB. Such reporting is the responsibility of OPM.

Contingencies

A contingency is an existing condition, situation, or set of circumstances involving uncertainty as to possible gain or loss. The uncertainty will ultimately be resolved when one or more future events occur or fail to occur. A contingent liability is recognized when a past event or exchange transaction has occurred, and a future outflow or other sacrifice of resources is measurable and probable. A contingency is disclosed in the Notes to the Financial Statements when any of the conditions for liability recognition are not met and the chance of the future confirming event or events occurring is more than remote but less than probable. As of September 30, 2014, the NTSB has a potential liability for approximately $400,000 related to claims where the probability of judgment is reasonably possible.

The NTSB is not a party to any legal actions that are likely to result in a material liability. Accordingly, no provision for loss is included in the financial statements.

Revenues and Other Financing Sources

Appropriations

Most of NTSB's operating funds are provided by congressional appropriations of budget authority. The NTSB receives appropriations on annual, multi-year, and no-year bases. NTSB receives financial resources from the following appropriations:

Annual Salaries and Expenses Appropriation

Annual one-year appropriations are provided by Congress and are available for obligation in the fiscal year for which it was provided to fund the overall operation of the NTSB.

Supplemental Salaries and Expenses Appropriation

Supplemental appropriations provided by Congress to fund extraordinary investigations.

Two Year Appropriation for Lease Renewal Expenses

For FY 2010, Congress appropriated $2,416,000 to fund one-time expenses associated with renewing the lease for NTSB's Washington, DC headquarters. The funding was available for obligation in FY 2010 and FY 2011.

Two Year Appropriation

For FY 2011 Congress appropriated $2.4 million. The funding was available for obligation in FY 2011 and FY 2012.

No Year Emergency Fund Appropriation

A no-year Emergency Fund appropriation was provided by the Congress to fund extraordinary accident investigation costs. Emergency Fund disbursements are made at the discretion of the NTSB, but must be reported to the Congress. A no-year appropriation is available for obligation without fiscal year limitation. The NTSB's Emergency Fund currently is appropriated at $1,997,884.

Imputed Financing Sources

In accordance with OMB Bulletin No. A-136, all expenses should be reported by agencies whether or not these expenses would be paid by the agency that incurs the expense. The amounts for certain expenses of the NTSB, which will be paid by other federal agencies, are recorded in the "Statement of Net Cost." A corresponding amount is recognized in the "Statement of Changes in Net Position" as an "Imputed Financing Source." These imputed financing sources primarily represent unfunded pension costs of NTSB employees.

Statement of Net Cost

Sub-Organization Program Costs
The NTSB Statement of Net Cost is presented by Responsibility Segment. These Responsibility Segments are based on the NTSB's mission and funding sources. The major programs that comprise the Responsibility Segments are: Aviation Safety, Surface Transportation Safety, and Research and Engineering.

Earned Revenue

Earned revenues collected by NTSB include amounts collected for training programs, rental of conference room space, subleasing of office space, and for investigative related services.

Net Position

Net position is the residual difference between assets and liabilities and comprises Unexpended Appropriations and Cumulative Results of Operations.

Unexpended appropriations include appropriations not yet obligated or expended, represented by the unobligated balances and undelivered orders of NTSB's appropriated funds. Multi-year appropriations remain available to NTSB for obligation in future periods. Unobligated balances associated with appropriations that expire at the end of the fiscal year remain available for obligation adjustments, but not for new obligations, until that account is closed, five years after the appropriations expire. Cumulative Results of Operations is the Net Result of NTSB's operations since inception.

Use of Estimates

The preparation of financial statements in accordance with the accounting principles described above requires management to make estimates and assumptions that affect the amounts reported in the financial statements and accompanying footnotes. Actual results could differ from those estimates.

Note 2

FUND BALANCES WITH THE U.S. TREASURY

U.S. Treasury processes NTSB cash receipts and disbursements. NonFederal receipts are deposited in commercial banks, which transfer the receipts to the U.S. Treasury. Funds with the U.S. Treasury represent appropriated funds and funds received in exchange for providing services. These funds are available to finance expenditures.

Fund Balance with the U.S. Treasury

Funds	Entity FY 2014	Non-Entity FY 2014	Total FY 2014	Entity FY 2013	Non-Entity FY 2013	Total FY 2013
Intragovernmental:						
Appropriated Funds	$ 36,210,047	$ -	$ 36,210,047	$ 34,233,150	$ -	$ 34,233,150
Unavailable Receipts	-	-	-	-	-	-
Total	$ 36,210,047	$ -	$ 36,210,047	$ 34,233,150	$ -	$ 34,233,150

Status of Fund Balance with Treasury	FY 2014	FY 2013
Unobligated Balance		
Available	$11,577,487	$6,983,308
Unavailable	7,435,639	9,850,927
Obligated Balance Not Yet Disbursed	17,196,921	17,398,915
Total	$36,210,047	$34,233,150

Note 3

ACCOUNTS RECEIVABLE

NTSB's accounts receivable represent amounts due from overpayments to current and non-current employees and from vendors. NTSB maintains an allowance for doubtful accounts for public receivables based on past collection experience. NTSB estimates the allowance for doubtful accounts based on the following agency schedule.

Days OUTSTANDING	PERCENTAGE
0-120	0%
Over 120 Days	100%

The allowance for doubtful accounts is reviewed and adjusted quarterly.

	Interagency FY 2014	Public FY 2014	Total FY 2014	Interagency FY 2013	Public FY 2013	Total FY 2013
Gross Receivables	$ -	$ 104,607	$ 104,607	$ -	$ 92,344	$ 92,344
Allowance for Loss	$ -	$ 90,502	$ 90,502	$ -	$ 91,910	$ 91,910
Net Receivables	$ -	$ 14,105	$ 14,105	$ -	$ 434	$ 434

Note 4

PROPERTY AND EQUIPMENT, NET

Property and equipment consisted of the following as of September 30, 2014 and 2013:

Property and Equipment

Classes of Fixed Assets	Service Life (Years)	Acquisition Value FY 2014	Accumulated Depreciation FY 2014	Net Book Value FY 2014	Acquisition Value FY 2013	Accumulated Depreciation FY 2013	Net Book Value FY 2013
Desktop and laptop computers and peripherals	3	$ 1,034,519	$ 545,996	$ 488,523	$ 1,034,520	$ 201,157	$ 833,363
Other ADP and Tele-comm equipment (servers, routers)	5	$ 294,723	$ 293,145	$ 1,578	$ 294,723	$ 261,941	$ 32,782
Furniture	5	$ 1,351,974	$ 917,382	$ 434,592	$ 1,351,973	$ 782,865	$ 569,108
Investigative equipment	5	$ 4,597,061	$ 3,578,451	$ 1,018,610	$ 2,541,352	$ 1,263,540	$ 1,277,812
Internal Use Software	3	$ 547,207	$ 309,013	$ 238,194	$ 2,178,105	$ 2,178,105	$ -
Leasehold Improvements	10	$ -	$ -	$ -	$ 628,163	$ 628,163	$ -
Capital lease (building)	20	$ 23,731,941	$ 13,152,456	$ 10,579,485	$ 23,731,941	$ 11,965,858	$ 11,766,083
Capital lease (Office Equipment)	5	$ 437,833	$ 211,579	$ 226,254	$ 437,833	$ 124,013	$ 313,820
Totals		$ 31,995,258	$ 19,008,022	$ 12,987,236	$ 32,198,610	$ 17,405,642	$ 14,792,968

Note 5

ACCRUED FECA LIABILITY

The Federal Employees' Compensation Act (FECA) provides income and medical cost protection to covered federal civilian employees injured on the job, employees who have incurred a work-related occupational disease, and beneficiaries of employees whose death is attributable to a job-related injury or occupational disease. Claims incurred for benefits for NTSB employees under FECA are administered by the Department of Labor (DOL) and are ultimately paid by the NTSB.

FECA liability includes two components: (1) the accrued liability which represents money owed for claims paid by the DOL through the current fiscal year, for which billing to and payment by the NTSB will occur in a subsequent fiscal year, and (2) the liability for future costs which represents the expected liability for approved compensation cases beyond the current fiscal year. Estimated future costs have been actuarially determined, and are regarded as a liability to the public because neither the costs nor reimbursement have been recognized by DOL. FECA liability is included in Liabilities Not Covered by Budgetary Resources, as described in Note 7.

The NTSB accrues liabilities based on estimates of funds owed to other federal government entities for services provided, but not yet billed. The accruals for Workers Compensation and Unemployment Compensation represent the estimated liability for the current fiscal year; for money owed, but not billed; and for claims, which were paid by the Department of Labor, but not yet billed to the NTSB.

Note 6

ACCRUED ANNUAL LEAVE

Accrued annual leave consists of employees' unpaid leave balances at September 30, 2014, and reflects wage rates in effect at quarter end. Accrued annual leave is included in Liabilities Not Covered by Budgetary Resources, as covered in Note 7.

Note 7

LIABILITIES COVERED AND NOT COVERED BY BUDGETARY RESOURCES

Liabilities Not Covered by Budgetary Resources result from the receipt of goods and services, or the occurrence of events, for which appropriations, revenues, or other financing sources necessary to pay the liabilities have not yet been made available through Congressional appropriation. These include FECA and annual leave liability. Unfunded Intragovernmental Liabilities consist solely of Accrued FECA in the amount of $1.3 million. Liabilities Covered by Budgetary Resources are those for which budgetary resources are available in the current fiscal year. NTSB's liabilities covered and not covered by budgetary resources are as follows:

Liabilities Covered and Not Covered by Budgetary Resources

Liabilities Covered by Budgetary Resources	FY 2014	FY 2013
Employer Contribution and Payroll Taxes Payable	$379,771	$315,747
Accounts Payable	1,594,266	707,022
Accrued Payroll	1,335,506	1,148,344
Capital Lease Liability	231,944	318,408
Total Liabilities Covered by Budgetary Resources	**$3,541,487**	**$2,489,521**
Liabilities Not Covered by Budgetary Resources		
Capital Lease Liability	13,597,198	14,770,420
Accrued Unfunded Annual Leave	5,225,303	5,032,830
Actuarial FECA Liability	7,042,672	7,139,580
Accrued Unfunded FECA Liability	1,271,101	1,315,868
Total Liabilities Not Covered by Budgetary Resources	**27,136,274**	**28,258,698**
Total Liabilities Covered and Not Covered by Budgetary Resources	**$30,677,761**	**$30,748,219**

Liabilities Covered and Not Covered by Budgetary Resources

Intragovernmental and Non-Intragovernmental

Intragovernmental		FY 2014		FY 2013
Accounts Payable	$	376,303	$	75,493
Other Liabilities		1,593,534		1,583,595
Total Intragovernmental	**$**	**1,969,837**	**$**	**1,659,088**
Accounts Payable	$	1,217,963	$	631,529
Accrued Payroll		1,335,506		1,148,344
Employer Contribution and Payroll Taxes Payable		57,338		48,020
Capital Lease Liability		13,829,142		15,088,828
Accrued Unfunded Annual Leave		5,225,303		5,032,830
Actuarial FECA Liability		7,042,672		7,139,580
Total Non-Intragovernmental		**28,707,924**		**29,089,131**
Total Liabilities Covered and Not Covered by Budgetary Resources	**$**	**30,677,761**	**$**	**30,748,219**

Note 8

LEASES

The NTSB has commitments under cancelable leases for office space. These leases have terms that extend up to 10 years. The majority of buildings in which the NTSB operates are leased from commercial companies. Under their lease agreement with the General Services Administration (GSA), the NTSB is charged rent that is intended to approximate commercial rental rates.

The NTSB has a 20-year capital lease for the Ashburn facility space which was entered into during 2001. The total future payments disclosed for the Ashburn facility include estimates for services and utilities.

The NTSB also has a 5-year capital lease for Lexmark copy machines which was entered into during 2012. The total future payments disclosed for the copy machines include estimates for service.

Future Capital Lease Payments

Fiscal Year	Space Rental FY 2014	Space Rental FY 2013
2014	$ -	2,694,985
2015	2,694,985	2,694,984
2016	2,694,984	2,694,984
2017	2,622,674	2,622,674
2018	2,521,440	2,521,440
2019	2,521,440	2,521,440
2020 and beyond	9,665,520	9,665,520
Total Future Lease Payments	**$22,721,043**	**$25,416,027**
Less: Imputed Interest	(3,507,419)	(4,275,003)
Less: Executory Costs (Maintenance)	(5,384,482)	(6,052,196)
Net Capital Lease Liability	**$13,829,142**	**$15,088,828**

In 2003 NTSB determined that the Ashburn facility lease should be recorded as a capital lease. Capitalizing the full net present value of the Ashburn facility lease created a deficiency in 2001 funds. This deficiency was reported to OMB and Congress. OMB has provided guidance on future funding and reporting of this liability. With the cancellation of the FY 2001 appropriation at September 30, 2006, the budgetary accounts no longer reflect a deficiency situation. The related asset, liability, and amortization will remain on the general ledger until the lease is fully liquidated. Annual Appropriation acts now include language to provide funds to make lease payments due in the current fiscal year.

The lease liability not covered by budgetary resources at September 30, 2014, is $13,597,198.

The NTSB has operating leases for postage meters and vehicles. Postage meters are leased on an annual basis. These leases are cancelable or renewable on an annual basis at the option of NTSB. They do not impose binding commitments on NTSB for future rental payments on leases with terms longer than one year.

Future operating payments due are as follows:

Future Operating Lease Payments at September 30, 2014

Fiscal Year	Space Rental-Headquarters and Regional Offices FY 2014		Space Rental-Headquarters and Regional Offices FY 2013
2014	$	-	8,651,222
2015		8,794,282	8,687,670
2016		8,863,150	8,733,909
2017		8,957,880	8,827,691
2018		9,055,447	8,924,287
2019		9,116,745	9,023,780
2020 and beyond		10,939,957	10,707,800
Total Future Lease payments	$	**55,727,461**	$ **63,556,359**

NTSB signed a new 10 year lease in August 2010.

GSA vehicle leases are cancelable at any time without penalty and are not included in Future Operating Lease Payments information.

Future Lease Receipts

In August 2007, NTSB signed a sub-lease agreement to provide certain office space beginning in September 2007.

This agreement is with the Transportation Security Administration (TSA) for a period of ten years beginning October 1, 2008. The Sub-Lessee may cancel this agreement after the first twelve months with 120 days' notice without penalty. This agreement will result in the receipt of $577,525 over the twelve-month lease term in accordance with amendment #6, paid quarterly. The Sub-Lessee rental rate will be annually adjusted by a reconciliation of Operating costs and taxes corresponding with increases to the Consumer Price Index (CPI) Cost of Living index.

Future Lease Receipts at September 30, 2014

Fiscal Year	TSA	
2015	$	577,525
2016		577,525
2017		577,525
2018		-
2019		-
2020 and beyond		-
Total Future Lease Receipts	$	**1,732,575**

Future Lease Receipts at September 30, 2013

Fiscal Year	TSA	
2014	$	597,746
2015		597,746
2016		597,746
2017		597,746
2018		-
2019 and beyond		-
Total Future Lease Receipts	$	**2,390,984**

Note 9

STATEMENT OF NET COST

Intragovernmental and Public Costs

Fiscal Year 2014	Aviation Safety	Surface Safety	Research & Engineering	Consolidated Totals
Intragovernmental Gross Costs	$ 14,672,643	$ 8,982,389	$ 7,968,862	$ 31,623,894
Less: Intragovernmental Earned Revenue	(444,029)	(186,510)	(165,465)	(796,004)
Intragovernmental Net Costs	$ 14,228,614	$8,795,879	$7,803,397	$30,827,890
Gross Costs with the Public	$ 36,388,087	$ 21,606,143	$ 14,583,453	$ 72,577,683
Less: Earned Revenues from the Public	(537,571)	(319,193)	(215,446)	(1,072,210)
Net Costs with the Public	$ 35,850,516	$ 21,286,950	$ 14,368,007	$ 71,505,473
Net Cost of Operations	**$ 50,079,130**	**$30,082,829**	**$ 22,171,404**	**$ 102,333,363**

Fiscal Year 2013	Aviation Safety	Surface Safety	Research & Engineering	Consolidated Totals
Intragovernmental Gross Costs	$ 14,800,608	$ 8,736,684	$ 5,386,815	$ 28,924,107
Less: Intragovernmental Earned Revenue	(422,948)	(224,442)	(138,385)	(785,775)
Intragovernmental Net Costs	$ 14,377,660	$8,512,242	$5,248,430	$28,138,332
Gross Costs with the Public	$ 39,096,564	$ 22,115,679	$ 15,688,010	$ 76,900,253
Less: Earned Revenues from the Public	(435,062)	(253,937)	(174,458)	(863,457)
Net Costs with the Public	$ 38,661,502	$ 21,861,742	$ 15,513,552	$ 76,036,796
Net Cost of Operations	**$ 53,039,162**	**$30,373,984**	**$ 20,761,982**	**$ 104,175,128**

Note 10

STATEMENT OF BUDGETARY RESOURCES

The Statement of Budgetary Resources compares budgetary resources with the status of those resources. For September 30, 2014, and September 30, 2013, respectively, budgetary resources were $121 million and $116 million; net outlays for the year were $97 million and $101 million; direct obligations incurred against amounts apportioned under Category A were $101 million and $98 million; and the amount of direct obligations incurred against amounts apportioned under Category B were $1 million and $1 million.

	FY 2014	FY 2013
Budgetary Resources	$121,147,411	$116,221,047
Net Outlays	96,909,174	101,169,264
Category A Apportionments	100,906,478	98,083,539
Reimbursable Category B	1,227,807	1,303,273

The total of undelivered orders at September 30, 2014, and 2013, were $13.7 million and $14.9 million.

Note 11

EXPLANATION OF DIFFERENCES BETWEEN THE STATEMENT OF BUDGETARY RESOURCES AND THE BUDGET OF THE UNITED STATES GOVERNMENT

FY 2013 Dollars in millions	Budgetary Resources	Obligations Incurred	Offsetting Receipts	Net Outlays
Statement of Budgetary Resources	$116	$99	$-	$101
Unobligated Balance Brought Forward	$(17)	-	-	-
Budget of the U.S. Government	$99	$99	-	$101
Differences	$-	$-	$-	$-

Source: Appendix, United States Budget

FY 2013 is the latest year for which actual figures are available. The President's Budget with actual figures for FY 2014 has not yet been published. Actual figures for FY 2014 are expected to be available in January 2015 and are expected to be found at http://www.whitehouse.gov/omb.

Note 12

NET COST OF OPERATIONS VS. BUDGET

	FY 2014	FY 2013
Resources Used to Finance Activities		
Obligations Incurred	$102,134,285	$99,386,812
Less: spending authority from offsetting collections and recoveries	(5,414,229)	(3,512,175)
Net obligations	96,720,056	95,874,637
Imputed financing from costs absorbed by others	3,702,585	3,464,443
Total resources used to finance activities	100,422,641	99,339,080
Resources Used to Finance Items not Part of the Net cost of operations		
Change in budgetary resources obligated for goods, services and benefits ordered but not yet provided	1,197,115	5,528,402
Resources that fund expenses recognized in prior periods	(1,304,453)	(1,241,824)
Resources that finance the acquisition of assets	(424,811)	(1,912,054)
Total resources used to finance items not part of the net cost of operations	(532,149)	2,374,524
Total resources used to finance the net cost of operations	$99,890,492	$101,713,604
Components of the Net Cost of Operations that will not require or generate Resources in the Current Period		
Other	212,328	305,019
Depreciation and Amortization	2,230,543	2,156,505
Total components of Net Cost of Operations that will not require or generate resources in the current period	2,442,871	2,461,524
Net Cost of Operations	$102,333,363	$104,175,128

For Additional Information Contact:

Edward Benthall
Chief Financial Officer

National Transportation Safety Board
Washington, DC 20594

cfofeed@ntsb.gov